ANIMALS ARE AMAZING

LIONS

BY VALERIE BODDEN

W
FRANKLIN WATTS
LONDON • SYDNEY

This edition published in the UK in 2014 by
Franklin Watts
338 Euston Road
London NW1 3BH

Franklin Watts Australia
Level 17/207 Kent Street
Sydney NSW 2000

First published by Creative Education,
an imprint of the Creative Company.
Copyright © 2010 Creative Education
International copyright reserved in all countries.
No part of this book may be reproduced in any
form without written permission from the publisher.

All rights reserved.

ISBN: 978 1 4451 2958 7
Dewey number: 599.7'57

A CIP catalogue record for this book
is available from the British Library.

Printed in China

Franklin Watts is a division of
Hachette Children's Books,
an Hachette UK company
www.hachette.co.uk

Book and cover design by The Design Lab
Art direction by Rita Marshall

Photographs by Getty Images (John Giustina, Beverly
Joubert, Stan Osolinski, Panoramic Images, Valerie
Shaff, Anup Shah, Paul Souders, Art Wolfe, Norbert
Wu), iStockphoto (David T. Gomez, Eric Isselée)

CONTENTS

What are lions?

Lions live in hot areas that have a lot of grass.

Lions are big cats. They are the second-largest cat in the world. The only cat that grows bigger than the lion is the tiger. There are only two **species** of lion in the world.

species different types of an animal that all share the same name.

Lion facts

This lion is showing off his deadly, sharp teeth!

Lions have a strong body that is covered with fur. The fur can be yellow or brown. Male lions have a mane. A mane is the area of bushy hair around the lion's head and neck. Lions also have a long tail, big teeth and very sharp claws!

A mane makes a male lion look even bigger.

Male and female lions

Male lions are stronger, but females are faster.

Male lions can grow to be 2.4 metres long. They can weigh more than two grown people! A female lion is a little smaller. She is called a lioness.

All lions can **roar**. It can be very loud. They roar to let other lions know where they are and to show how big and strong they are.

roar the loud, scary noise that a lion can make.

Where lions live

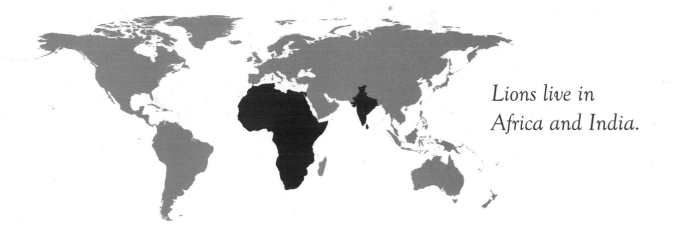

Lions live in Africa and India.

Most lions live on the **continent** of Africa. This is why they are called African lions. The area they live in is called the **savanna**. The other species of lion lives in India. They are called Asiatic (*ay-zhe-AT-ick*) lions. They live in a place called the Gir Forest.

continent one of Earth's seven big pieces of land.
savanna flat, hot land covered with grass and a few trees.

Lion food

A lion can eat 34 kilogrammes of meat in one meal.

Lions are **carnivores**; they eat other animals. Some of their favourite animals to eat are zebras, wildebeest and antelopes. Sometimes lions eat elephants. A few lions have even eaten people!

carnivore an animal that only eats meat.

New lions

Female lions keep a careful watch over all the cubs.

A mother lion gives birth to between two and six **cubs** at a time. At first, the cubs stay in a **den** with their mother. Cubs are born with their eyes shut. Their eyes open after about one week and they leave the den when they are five weeks old. They begin to learn how to hunt by playing with each other. Lions in the wild can live for 15 years.

cubs baby lions.
den a home that is hidden, like a cave.

Pride life

Lions live in family groups called prides. Most prides have about 15 lions: one big male lion and lots of females and cubs. Prides also have one or two young male lions. They live with the pride until they are 2 or 3 years old. Then they leave and start prides of their own.

Adult lions spend a lot of time sleeping. About 20 hours each day! Cubs like to play and chase small animals.

Lions like to rest during the hottest part of the day.

Hunting for food

*Lions often look for sick or
old animals to catch and eat.*

Lions often hunt at night. They can sneak up on their **prey** more easily in the dark. But lions also hunt during the day. Female lions do most of the hunting. They usually work together as a team. They use their teeth and claws to kill their prey. The male lions get to eat first. The females and cubs have to wait until the males have finished eating.

prey an animal that is eaten by other animals.

Lions and people

Today, people around the world can go to zoos or safari parks to see lions. Some people even go to Africa or Asia to see lions in the wild. It is exciting to get close to these big cats!

Zoo lions and wild lions like to spend time playing.

A lion story

Why do lions roar? People in Africa tell a story about this. They say that the lion used to sneak up on animals and eat them. One day, a **hare** put honey from a beehive on the lion while he slept. When the bees saw the honey, they stung the lion. The pain made the lion roar. From then on, the lion roared – and the animals always heard him coming!

hare an animal that looks like a rabbit but is bigger.